All This and More

All This and More

New and Selected Poems

Carol Connolly

NODIN PRESS

Cover art: Phyllis Wiener
Cover Design: Maria Mazzara
Book layout: John Toren

ISBN: 978-1-932472-93-6

Library of Congress Control Number: 2009936286

Nodin Press, LLC
530 N. Third Street, Suite 120
Minneapolis, MN
55401

A deep bow to the women and men who inspired these poems, and to the late great Meridel LeSueur and Rachel Tilsen, who first brought this work to print. Grateful applause, as well, to Oprah Winfrey, Gail Sheehy, Carolyn Holbrook, Sally Child, Gloria Calomee, Kathryn Altman, and to so many others, whose generosity and talent have given this work life and voice.

CONTENTS

THE MUSIC OF WHAT IS

FOREWORD

It's no mere coincidence that these poems are doing what almost no poems do. It was not sheer luck that Oprah Winfrey chose to read from Connolly's work on her television show, or that two theatrical producers, one in Los Angeles, and one in Minneapolis, successfully presented these poems in full length staged productions. These productions ran for two seasons in each city.

Carol Connolly's poetry speaks directly and clearly. This elegant woman writes poems that are funny and gritty and honest, and it's quite impossible not to find your own life and feelings in what she says. The poems are tiny brain-drillings, opening mind-gushers of recognition and revelation for their readers. They are a joy and they're definitely for adults only. That makes them dangerous. Write your name in this book as almost surely you're going to want to pass it on to a friend. Tell them your new friend Carol Connolly wrote it and that it's time for a little danger and humor in their lives, not to mention beauty.

– Steve Kaplan, Editor
Law & Politics: Only Our Name is Boring

#359 09-25-2022 01:32PM
Item(s) checked out to p1031779.

TITLE: The wife
BC: 32091049351415
DUE: 10-23-22

TITLE: Wire in the blood. Season 2 [vide
BC: 32091063613210
DUE: 10-23-22

TITLE: Modernist women poets : an anthol
BC: 32091048257373
DUE: 10-23-22

TITLE: Given : new poems
BC: 32091034791500
DUE: 10-23-22

TITLE: All this and more : new and selec
BC: 32091040411242
DUE: 10-23-22

Phone Renewal is Back!
Renew or check your account 651-292-6002

HAT FIRST

On the Study of Mythology

When, at last, she took
a good look at Medusa,
she began to understand.

A man can be
in terror of a woman.
Buried in his marrow

is the ancient fear
of falling slowly
into her dark recesses,

tumbling
rolling
disappearing

part by part,
hat first,
until all that remains

is one wing-tip oxford,
shoelace dangling
on the white sheet.

Have You Ever Loved an Ugly Man?

All real lovers know
desire is a mystery.
You can be moved by
a voice
a form
a kind of smile
sometimes by
a name
a family name
the curve of a back
the angle of a hat or
a certain pomposity.
A phrase.
Some unexpected vulgarity.
All of it can add up
or come down
to a man
who, by all
the usual standards,
might be regarded
as a monster.

Distance at Close Range

The man whose mind is on safari,
even as his body feeds
at your table, even as he moves

up and down in your bed,
this is the man who blames you
as he packs a bag

and heads for a strange room overnight,
says it's your fault
as he dives straight

into one whiskey and then another.
Risks drowning
rather than fight it out.

About who said what.
About who owes what.
About who loves who.

You acquiesce to the intricacies of his
every demand. To appease him, you choose
drab colors. Wear a hat. In silence

you grow frantic. Seek comfort
in or after or outside
his trail of debris,

do your best to stuff it into sacks,
sweep the path behind you.
Make it smooth.

This is the man. And you, you are
caught in a cocoon of your own spinning
long after he forsakes you

to absent himself
at a second table,
in a third bed.

What If

A woman with thick ankles knows early
that she has no power

What if a pebble hits my windshield
and continues on
through my
left eye, or
what if you write a hit song
and leave me for a blond
girl with slender legs,
tan like bamboo, or
write a hit play
and leave me for a blond
boy with slender legs,
tan like bamboo, or
what if your oil well gushes
and you
leave me for
a cowgirl.

What if you leave and never return,
and, worse,
what if you return
and never leave.
I fear being alone, but
what if I tell you that
even more
I fear never being alone.
You say your vows are true.
You hold me, murmur low,
promise me stars,
but where will you be tomorrow?
What if I can't find a place to park?

What I Know About Money

He stops
what you count on the most.
You reel from the shock.

You want him dead.
But the air he breathes out,
you breathe in.

You move slowly
through a crowd of shadows,
begin a frantic search

for clean air.
You find an expert. He wears
a Harley Davidson cap. He rides

a wheelchair. He says
get your anxiety
into the mail stream

before midnight,
or your oxygen, he says,
will not, he says,

be delivered in time.
You begin to gasp, to add,
subtract, grind out four

or more petitions every hour.
You try not to hallucinate.
You gyrate. You punctuate.

You get help with the syntax,
change the verbs again and again,
desperate for a balance

you exhale and blow red
ink into the setting sun.
You know where the bottom line is

and just before dark
you slip over.
The silence is deafening.

You give birth
to terror
one limb at a time

breathe in, breathe in, and when
you collapse in a heap of your own errors,
a janitor sweeps in

to hang the blue and gold banner
of the Optimists, who will gather
when you leave.

Late Date at LeZinc

On the third day
of the third month,
after a week of greetings

and partings
in places polluted
with dangerous decibels,

we meet to part.
The same old shrimp,
antennae paralyzed,

stare once more
from your white plate.
Metal music bounces

off the zinc bar,
hits the tin ceiling,
shows no mercy.

I want you to understand,
I shout. I don't blame you,
I shriek. I forgive myself,

I shout, as you drown
in the pounding waves
of a stranger in a silly hat

at the next table
Her every syllable
is audible.

She decribes her
manicure to her
companion. His

hat is in his
hand. I flounder.
You pale, nail by nail.

Slick Road

It started out to be
a halfway decent day.
I hear news of you
and the freezing rain
predicted for dusk
begins at noon.
The radio issues a warning,
hang on to your hat,
and a man's voice
authoritative as hell
speaks of the dangers
of swine dysentery.
On this slick road
trees out of leaf
lean across the horizon
lift their gnarled arms
form an intricate net
and keep me from
skidding slipping sliding slowly
off the edge.

BALANCING ACT IN MIDLIFE

The moon is high. Your bronze
satin would shimmer
in this abnormal heat,
sweat rosebuds as you move
your hands, your mouth.

You vow this
intense new
moonlight
blinded you
at first sight.

I watch the leaves on my tree
turn purple slowly. It is
October, time for harvest,
and you are in the bayou.
My hat is tethered here.

We do the great moonbeam
balancing act,
juggle the brilliance
between us. My hand
is steady when you call.

You say the leaves
on all the trees
in your town
have been purple
for some time now.

The Future is a Blinding Mirage

Time and time again he pushed her aside.
Sometimes she slipped to the floor.
Once she bled a little on the Chinese rug.
He raged about the stain. Somehow
she stepped around it, grabbed her hat.
He pushed her harder. This time she falls,

catches her head on the edge
of a glass cocktail table, knows at once
her skull is ripped. Pain
sears her core, her gaping wound
oozes, her hair puffs dark, begins
to mat under her hat. The police say

she needs help. The surgeon says
he won't touch her, he says
her hat isn't clean, he says
he can always smell a lawsuit
in this home-blown kind of storm.
She brought this on herself, he says.

Slowly, she sees she must abandon
her hat, her coat, push past the surgeon,
past the orderlies who lock arms,
make a barricade, shake their fingers,
and warn her. Do not
take that raw wound outside

these locked doors. Snow falls
thick and fast. She slips, slides,
careens, and slowly, so slowly,
catches her balance
and begins to glide,
never smoothly, but very surely,

she escapes
into the blizzard's
mystical
magical
brand new beauty.

WIND CHILLED-TOWN

You come to me from the steamy mist
of a torrid zone,
but you are
gone
before you arrive. Still,

I hear your voice when
I comb my hair, the faint roll
of your *r*. You say
there is something strange
between us. You say

there is a fleck of deep
purple in my eye. You say
you don't give a damn
about New Orleans. You say
you only want to be

in my wind-chilled town.
I wait in black and white
intensity.
My hand is on my heart.
I wait to hear you sing

tunes of totems,
tell tales of triumphs.
I wait to savor every
succulent syllable. You
swagger in. Your hat

is flat. Your song is boiled
to a stale, familiar mush.
I wait now, I wait, I wait
for you to leave.
I want to disappear.

GOODBYE
– for Dorothy Parker

I wouldn't like to be
the Queen of Romania,
rule the land or stand
in ceremony, serene
in the face of confusion,
but I would, yes,
I would like to see
the Queen of Romania
sitting straight
in the first box
at the new World Theatre,
her hat scrolled in gold,
ornate as the pillars
supporting her pedestal.
I would stare at her,
savor every detail.
I would, yes,

I would like to leave
him slumped
in the balcony
and sit close
to the Queen of Romania,
face forward, hear
the music, clutch
my pocketbook and walk
with the Queen of Romania
to the exit.
I would, yes,
I would wave
graciously
as he disappears
through a hole
in the night.

MAN'S BEST FRIEND

In the center
of the Empire
men dress in fine ensembles
and walk the dog.
They bend beneath curbs,
gather warm dog excrement
in clear bags pulled
from fine silk pockets.
Only the finest.
This is the center
of the Empire,
where money
talks
and dogs are walked
on Gucci leashes
and dog dirt
is collected.
E is for Empire.
Its excellence
is elegant,
but excrement
exists.
In piles.

I Won't
— for Cynthia

If in winter, he drops you
in mid-flight, dead center
into the deep, dark sea,
and you can't swim,
you will be shocked.
Your blood will run cold.

You will drag yourself to shore,
clutch your sides, shiver, sputter,
struggle for air, stand slowly
and gasp that you are
hideously disillusioned.
Passersby will tell you

you brought it on yourself.
How could you
trust that schmuck,
and then you pledge:
I don't.
I don't. I won't.

Sometime later
when the light is right
he will come around
yet again
with talk
of another uncharted flight.

Now you will have enough air
to burst into a no oh no
I won't I will not
go up with you again.
Then he will put on his hat,
turn his face from you

and mumble, my god.
You are a cold piece.
Maybe even
frigid.

Without a Hat

If you are
not a blessed virgin
but an ordinary woman
full of ordinary dreams
on an ordinary night,
full of wine and expectation
when the moon is high,
you might find a handsome athlete
and dance slow with him,
sway a little to his song,
and go with him
for just a little while.
But should he gather others,
make an all-American trio
who lock you with their
music in a plain room,
taunt you
and ridicule you
as they abuse you,
take their turns
all night, all night,
at hurting you so bad,
so bad,
all that will remain in you is
one scream
and you will cry
for help.
Help.
Then you will be required
in extraordinary ways,
again and yet again,
to explain
why you
are just an ordinary woman
and not a blessed virgin.

Fast Shadows

She is seated in ceremony,
taps her fingers on the table,
casting fast shadows
on the cafe's linen cloth,
every fiber stretched white.
She slowly crosses her legs.
Never will they know again
the weight of her husband's body.
He abandoned her without notice.
Gave in to a failing heart
on a tennis court in Mexico.
They were there to outwit
the white of winter.
Now once more
she uncrosses her long white widow's legs
and feels the weight
of the quiet loneliness of solitude,
waits for the arrival
of a new man she knows but little.
Stares.
Contemplates cockroaches
and dreads their fast shadows,
the way they appear and disappear
in silence
without notice.

HELP

The man at my side
at dinner, in a fine café,
wears very chic clothes
strikes a fine pose,
and just before coffee,
picks his nose.
His idiosyncrasies
are exposed.
I never supposed
I would have to propose
a fig leaf.
All you people passing by,
holding your noses sky high,
this man is naked.
Can't you help me?
Hand the man his hat.

GRATITUDE

When the light is right,
the sweet perfume of hyacinths
rolls around me.

I say thanks to everyone
but myself.

I bow low to my mother
buried in 1959,
to my father

buried on the same day,
to my brother
who moved to Edina,

to a husband
who had the good sense
to divorce me,

to my children
who followed nature
and grew up,

to the man in a hat
who says he adores me,
to the men who say nothing.

When the sky is dark at noon
and all the hyacinths
are dead and dank,

I blame no one
but myself.

FLAG DAY

Sworn to brand new
loyalties,
the Hmong major
sports a neon blue
team jacket.
A red cap,

at a rakish angle,
shadows
the wide stripes
of his struggle,
of his longing
for his lost homeland.

His headset plays
a rhythm he obeys.
He bounces through
the grocer's aisles,
salutes the baker's rack
piled high with Wonder Bread,

and stops flat.
Taps his pocket Sony,
keeps the beat,
and in brand new
C sharp American, raps

"Hey, they don't
have no
apple pie.
They do not
have no apple pie."

REJECTION

No thanks for your work,
the editor says.
This requires
two typewritten pages.
Cut your poems
up, he says.
Line by line, he says.
Put the lines together in a hat.
Pull them out,
one at a time
and see what happens.

Ah, but
I don't
have a hat.

DILETTANTE

I am a full-time fraud,
passing as a poet.
It's filthy work. But
someone has to do it.
Stilted syllables
line my walls,
confusion
crowds my room
with maggoty mounds
of mediocre metaphors,
ridicule lurks
in my hallway,
ambitious people
take all the best lines,
and I have a headache.
I woke up with it. But
everyone wakes up
with something.

MULTIPLICATION

Stacks of paper layered on my desk
toss and turn and after midnight
do a strange dance of procreation,
become fruitful and multiply.
They are here to stay,
but the poem I read to shreds,
the poem that saved me
when the speeding Acura
jumped a red light at 95th Street,
struck him, threw him sky high,
mutilated his body
mangled his brain
flattened his Panama hat,
that poem has gone missing.
I didn't protect it.
I didn't keep it safe.
I thought dumping every remnant
of those early weeks punctuated
with tubes and pulsating machines
intensive care and dire predictions
would surely ease him back
into our happy lives.
It was an exercise in futility.
Those dire predictions
shadow him. Grow darker.
He searches incessantly now
for his Panama hat left bloodied
on the curb at 95 and Third.
I search for the poem I cannot say.
Can you? Or have you, like me,
lost it.

DEEP IN THE WOODS

Spread this upon the minutes:
All trauma is in the present.
The findings of fact say it's over.
You have been ravished.
You are ordered to shoot the horses.
You are ordered to burn the barn.
You are ordered to move on.
You have no discretion in this matter.
You can refuse, but the fact remains.
You are now obstacle dominated.
You do, however, have full permission
to ask any questions you wish
of your lawyer.

Learned counsel,
where did you
get that hat?

No Vacancy

Riding all night
past neon signs that blink
No vacancy.
Closed. No eggs for travelers.
Meeting dawn in a mountain town.
In small houses
close to the road
daily rituals are observed.
Coffee is cooking,
women crack eggs,
men shave in silence,
children stretch and yawn
on the edge of rumpled beds.
I am on the road.
Before the sun brings noon,
I'll stretch my legs
in New York City.
Tomorrow is as fragile
as a sheer curtain pulled tight.
Any old dog
who comes along
can put his paw
through it.

LEAVING
– for Eden

During his month-long coma,
experts advised me to speak to him,
to tell him, if he didn't wish to suffer
this endless brutality, this residue
of a speeding hit and run, his
broken bones, his broken head,
if he wanted to move on
to the next world, each of us
who stood at his side would
understand. I did as I was told.
I stood by him day after long
sad day and repeated: If you
don't wish to suffer this, if you
want to leave, I will love you
forever. You can leave, if you
want to leave, if that is your
wish, to leave, you may leave.
When he came to, jubilation
broke out in the halls
of that Manhattan hospital.
His first words?

Sweetheart.
It is glorious to see you.
I plan to leave tomorrow.
I will need a coat and hat.

ROMANCE

In every romance
there is a time, early,
when I want to consume him,
own him,
lock him in a closet in my vicinity.
A closet with a window.
I am not a killer.
I want to put him in a box,
carry him with me,
and if he, without looking,
steps into the box,
I close the cover quickly,
bang it shut,
and hang it with a heavy padlock.

As I turn the key in the lock,
I look at him curled in the box
and think,
"You idiot. What are you doing in that box?"

SEEING RED

RED

One warehouse window painted red.
One aged caboose, faded red, meanders

alone across a high trestle.
One red rage doll waits to be stuffed.

Her maker will finish her
urge me to ignore its human form

pummel the doll beat her
slam her against a red tile floor.

I cannot. I will keep my rage
to myself. I hear it pecking,

this bird on the roof I cannot see.
I am always aware of its red presence.

Sometimes it spreads its wings,
casts a shadow over me. Stuck.

Idling at the corner. Pleading
for the light to change from red.

An Apple

In a bittersweet room,
even the blinds were red,
we moved from the heat
of the setting sun
into each other's arms
in a liaison as illicit
as it was inescapable.
Without choosing, we chose
to float on the surf
of that downtown shore,
our limbs drenched
with fire,
red in the last light
of the circling sun.
Afterwards, in the quiet,

he paid the hotel bill,
as men do in these cases.
I paid the price,
as women do.

THE INTRUDER

He chugs in, covered with sweat
and confusion, expects me
to draw a bath. Clean him up.
Serve espresso. Perk things up.

Press his pants. Better yet,
would I lend him a red silk gown?
Absurd and inappropriate,
he expects me

to ignore this oppressive heat,
brace up against his sweat,
give form to the demands
of his awkward grace,

this bond between us.
I am a weary quack.
I sharpen my tools once more
and agree. I will surrender.

I will do what I must to rescue him,
pull a poem from his confusion,
knowing all the while
that as soon as I do,

he will pack his bag
and move on, leaving me
to worry and to wonder.
Will we ever meet again?

ALL SEASONS

I was determined
to find
a substitute for you

knowing that past 40
we are, each of us,
a substitute for someone.

I pledged to a husband, a lover,
and then to a younger lover,
who dances with wild abandon,

but when you surface,
from the deep well of absence,
your dark eyes steaming,

I know once more,
any such pledge is futile.
Forever

I am linked
to your mad intensities,
your long legs.

A Gentleman's Invitation

Meet me at six o'clock
at the New French Cafe.
We will share,
says he,
a cup of consomme.
Handsome is he
and debonair.
His smile is as wide
as the English Channel.
But a hungry woman
searching for substance
could
drown
in a cup of consomme
at six o'clock
at the New French Cafe.

April

Eavesdropping these days is worthless.
In the small cafes, even the poets
talk of taxes. Deductions,
how to snare them. Capital gains,
how to ignore them.

It's April. Here in the North,
the weather careens between summer
and the moon's death hold on winter.
It bullies the budding trees.
The tax man bullies me.

I dig through stacks of rumpled files
for fodder to appease his enormous
appetite for piles of paper marred
with nonsensical numbers. I think
I'll pack a bag and flee.

I could escape to Menomonie
or, better yet, get lost in Las Vegas,
but, where is Frank Sinatra?
I whine. I sulk.
I have no one to bully.

It's April everywhere.

Below Zero

Dangerous weather.
Windchill
sixty-five degrees
below zero.
I tell you I have seen, just now,
on the freeway leading from Minneapolis,
thirteen cars stalled,
five cars in one wreck,
and a sports car descending,
taillights in a spiral,
over the edge of a bridge.

You say "My god,"
the whine of ridicule in your voice,
"life and death within a mile,
a veritable working girl's Vietnam,"
as though the only
valid experience,
this weather, is yours.

Do I still love you?
It's like riding a bicycle.
If I begin again,
I'll be able to do it.

THE TALL MAN
   – for Eugene J. McCarthy

The tall man steps from a jet plane
in from that far land where prophets live
alone. I embrace him, as I always do,
but this time I hang on. Bury my head
in the shoulder of his dark blue suit.
He says, we are spiraling down.
I say, I know.

Anything can happen now.
The world seems off its axis,
even our grown children
are not perfect,
and our deep bruises,
now decades old,
are still dark blue.

The sun must set and the red moon
rests on the edge of the world, slipping
ever lower before it disappears.
The tall man grows frail, his age demands it,
and I don't see the wisdom in any of this.
If I had an old dog, I would call her now
and scratch behind her ears.

Heat

After the relentless heat
of a long dry summer,
the horizon blazes
the color of endings.
A hard wind blows,
soon the trees are out of leaf,
and one morning your
rooms, like mine, are cold.
You push a switch.
You feel the heat rise,
and your belief
in the god of your
childhood is restored.
All the little losses
knotted up in your heart
begin to loosen and unravel.
The one who disturbs you
stops calling,
and a soft rain
begins.

Noise

I am out of words.
The radio, set to start the day,
plays a piano's perfect sonata,
wakes me to a silent house.
The man who composed sonatas
and played the piano here
is gone. Now
I live with quiet.
I have no music. No words.
I decide to cook,
to clang and bang
pots and pan lids
make a big red noise
upset the quiet,
but what one does alone
is often so small.
In the silent pantry, I slam
through stacks of cookbooks.
I need a recipe for weeping.
I am out of words.

Silence

Enough words. Talking
is a mess. A jumbled clutter
full of pitfalls, potential disaster.
You speak a few thoughtless
words and they blink blink neon
bright for decades. Haunt you,
remain ever faithful to their
mission never to be unplugged.
I will keep silence now
in the ancient manner
that fortified cloistered nuns.
My vow will allow me
to breathe in and out,
but nothing more.
Silence has been proven
to be useful. In a crowd,
it removes you
from the fray, makes you
as mysterious as Mata Hari.
When you are alone, it fills
your rooms with order.
Talking is a mess.

TRUCKING

I find I am attracted now
to the snouts of shiny trucks.
Their polished grilles
smile wide as they approach,
chrome teeth gleam as they
sweep by in the slow steamy
heat of late afternoon sun.
Bold and brave and full
of grace they sway easily
in and out of snarled traffic.
Yesterday, a red Bronco in my rear
view mirror came menacingly close,
then moved on
wanting nothing of me
but a moment's notice.

It is natural to search
for a mate. To seek.
To find. To not be resigned. I am
past the breeding stage of life.
I find I am attracted now
to the snouts of shiny trucks.

FANTASY

– for the president's aide

If my breasts were,
as he said,
as sharp and pointed
as the pyramids,
I would use them
to cut
red x's
in his face.

Hit and Run

Hang on, fold the corners tight,
put all unopened mail in a basket far
under your desk, accept every
invitation, go everywhere, look
attentive, but don't listen when they
talk of their successes, their growing
bank accounts, their love, their new,
their improved, and don't mention
what is hanging, always, in the very
front of your mind. Despite all your
efforts to shrink it, stuff it, stifle it,
your grief is ever growing.
Keep all conversation in safe
territory, doors locked, double
bolted, and maybe, just maybe,
you will make it through the day
without exposing your nightmare,
the smashed windshield, the blood
in the street, the gore, the gore,
his broken body, his busted brain,
and you will not, you will not, sob
openly over the loss of your happy life.
You will continue to struggle
to accommodate the new
and difficult days that loom
like a burial, or perhaps
you are already dead,
strangled by the terrible
presence of his absence.

THE TYRANNY OF ZERO

The sun is a bare bulb hanging
from the peeling paint of a January sky.
The wind is dancing a slow reel
with a thin snow. My windows
are iced with hills and valleys,
an intricate assemblage of rectangles
resembling the grid of a distant city.
Any city. I want to be there,
with you, away from this weather.

You are trapped here with your balance
gone, wrecked by an Acura Legend
that missed a red light,
found you, and took your memory.
I am trapped here by your loss,
which has become mine.
The truth stands silent between us,
at attention, heels of its worn
shoes pressed together.

Our bags are packed.
We are going nowhere.

The Flaw

Each morning I move
my magnifying mirror
to a window sill
and think of you.
Capture the red sun

and pull out
some unwanted sprout
that has taken up space
on my face
as I slept and turned

with dreams of you that appear
uninvited in the dark.
I have not seen your face
in so many years the exact, in fact,
number of years through which

we adored each other,
madly, and with passion.
Is that true?
Or was it just
that I adored you.

My Sisters

When madness descends,
wraps itself around my legs,
begins to paralyze me,
you, my sisters, hold me
on this side of the fine line
that divides sunlight
from insanity.
You are spring
to my frozen field.
Summer rain
to my drought.
You are the moon
in my dark night.
Your resolute wisdom
surrounds me
in circles that ripple wide
and hold my daughters
and their daughters
in a place where
the sun shines bright,
and strength blooms,
steadfast in its beauty.

C Shape

If you think I am
in a dark place
here in the heartland
curled in a C shape
wrapped in
sighs like red silk
hidden from
the light of Human Kindness
lonely and yearning
for the Black Magic
in your eyes,
you are dead wrong.

I only weep when
I am alone on the
highway that never,
no never,
takes me home.

CAFFEINE CRAZY AT CARIBOU

A mind
is a terrible
thing to taste and yours
is spilling over into my cold
coffee

murky
matter too thick
to swallow it gurgles
up and over out of my cup
rumbles

bubbles
up and slips over
onto my white knuckles
lopes along and oozes over
table's edge

drops
to my stone thighs,
my bent knees and slides slow
down my legs, pushes into my
loose red shoes.

When I
leave you, and I
will, I will slog away
on soggy soles no new wind will
whistle dry.

HARVEST

She gives a long soliloquy
in a light redundant monotone
about how
she chose a perfect husband
about how
it was no accident
about how
her precocious wisdom
has been proven right
time and time again.
Time and time again.
She preens and puffs
cheeps in celebration
for her impeccable judgment
about how
a lifelong pairing
is the only thing.
Everything.

He sits red-eyed and silent
dwindled to a short bundle
of dried corn stalks
propped up and bound
by the endless
twine of her words
about how.

FAST DANCE

The question,
"Have you ever been married?"
is a yellow taxi
screaming through a red light.

I jump aside. I take a dive
into a pickle barrel.
My weak flesh fills
its dark void.

There is no music,
but I dance fast and wild
until the pickle barrel
bursts. Brine

salty as tears
sputters into the gutter.
I rise from the debris
and murmur

the answer:
Yes. I have been married.
But, I was never truly married
to the man I married.

KIERAN DOHERTY

You come at your death
from your birth in a Catholic ghetto.
You take some time to read, to sing.
You learn to lay brick,
and then you join
the forty percent of your kind
who find no work in Ulster.
You are Irish.

Early one morning a building explodes.
You are nearby.
You suffer arrest and conviction
under a judge appointed by your enemy
without benefit of a jury of your peers.
You have no right to appeal.
You had no hand in choosing
this government that rules you
and it has Special Powers.

In H block, in Her Majesty's prison,
you clench your fists,
and take up the ancient banner
of your people, who from the beginning,
fasted on the doorstep of a transgressor
until justice or death was done.

You oppose your enemy
with the last weapon you have.
You heave your life at the oppressor.
You hunger after justice
until death.

People gather on the steps
of St. Patrick's to pray.

A woman in a purple suit,
nails enameled red, shouts rubbish
at your mourners.

The *New York Times* says you are
morbid to fast when a Prince
is being married to a 19 year old virgin.
After all, this is a time
when virgins are hard to find,
and you are spoiling the party.

People who know about such things,
who understand history
and are vigilant about freedom
will sing your plain song
around the world,
and they will teach its melody
to their children and their children's children
for all the generations to come.

The Joy of Fear

The big man in the next seat stashes
his ten gallon hat and confesses.
His scale weighs five pounds heavy.
His Rolex is set five minutes fast.

High above drought-plagued Dallas
just as the city begins
to light the red night sky,
just as people on the ground

sit down in saloons and living rooms,
the jet plane hits a hole and tumbles.
The big man in the next seat mumbles
into his Jim Beam. If he goes down,

we all go down.
Five minutes won't matter.
Five pounds won't matter.
Being brave just this once

will matter,
that the truth is so
easily lost
will matter.

SHALLOWS

– For the 577 demonstrators arrested at Honeywell

I want to float in the shallow water
close to the shore
where the sea is still,
the sand is white.

I want to loll
on my back on a puffed-up life raft,
search for the silver lining,
gaze at the sky as blue as blue,

glide straight into the sun,
and be consoled.
Never look back.
I have been in deep water.

I could
tell you stories
you would not
believe.

I will be alone now,
solitary, celibate.
I don't want to hear even a whisper
of the syllables in nuclear,

the hiss in holocaust,
the murder in mutilation.
I don't want to smell the sweat
in demonstrate or lobby or elect.

The kingfishers will roar by
in speedboats.
I won't even wave.

Far in the distance
the heat shimmers.
You may decide
to board a big boat,
chain your body to a war machine.

Remove all sharp objects
from your pockets
so you won't hurt yourself
or wound the cop who arrests you.

The steel door will bang behind you.
The jailor will say your time begins.
Keep in mind,
what is legal is not,

and as you pour strength
into the deep ocean
that floats my raft close to the shore,
I will be safe in the sun

because you
hold back the dark
with your bare hands.

Manhattan Fever

Pulled to a stone wall
by the shimmer of Central Park

in heat unexpected
on the last day of March,

lured by splashes of forsythia,
green escaping red

bud skins and moist ground
charmed by the pond,

its dark still water. I could
step forever into its silence,

but the fear of loneliness,
foreboding of the boredom

that comes sometimes
with quiet, pulls me

back to the line of yellow taxis
gleaming in the morning sun,

waiting to speed on
to Seventh Avenue

in obedience to the savage
pull of commerce.

GRAFFITI

On the Double A Train
Saint Miter
and his Roman numerals
slump
nearly buried
in a dark jumble
3/N One Ding Ding
Porn Con
Lexie Z
Murder.

At 51st Street
I trade my morning
for your whitewashed walls,
stand in your shadow,
until it swallows my afternoon,
and from 9 to 5 sidestep the dark jumble
of your confusion.
I guard the scream
trapped in my flesh.
I guard it fiercely.
If it escapes, it will wrap red
around your neck
past you to her
and on to him
pulling tighter tighter
tighter as it winds.

One Ding Ding
Porn Con
Lexie Z.
Murder.

RADICAL ACTS

Sometimes I iron pillowcases.
Not because it's important.
Not because it creates a cure,
saves the planet, or saves a life.
I iron because I know how
to do it. I do it well.
It's a comfort in these dot.com days,
when so much is so mysterious,
to simply, with a sure hand,
glide a red hot iron back
and forth across clean cotton.
Make the wrinkles disappear.
It's a comfort when a young
woman with a shiny new
degree says, I don't get this,
and tell me again:
Who is Gloria Steinem?
It's a victory then,
without the interference
of my own ignorance,
or the stupidity of others,
to steam a perfect crease.
Sometimes, I go so far as to
iron handkerchiefs.

Between Trains
– for Carrie

She lives her life as though
she were between trains.
Her bags are never unpacked.
She memorizes every express
schedule, knows the exact time
of all westbound departures
and she is careful. Careful
to never be far from a phone.
She waits for some word,
any word will do,
from her tall blond beloved.
He lives in the sun
with his work.
She endures winter.
Her red dress shimmers
as the short man at her side
brings her peaches in March,
tells her he is hers forever.
She stands on one foot,
tapping the other,
waiting to travel.
Her eye is on the coast.

THE POOL

Clean the pool, they said.
Float lilies. Raise one fish,
one dancing fish that will
glitter as it reflects the light.
Make you rich
in your old age.
You thought a clean pool
was not that important.
Now schools of unsavory fish
roam your scummy water,
red fish with protruding eyes,
old fish that have hung
on for years, dying fish
stinking, rotting, sick fish.
They have folded the lilies flat.
Cleaning the pool is not enough
now. You beg for help,
borrow shovels, wheelbarrows,
trucks, until you understand.
You have become a prisoner
of your own fiction,
flinging your net,
thinking you can rescue
your one dancing fish.
You are too late.

LAMENT

I want to know
how the blind man
will open a milk carton.
I long for a wide vista
a clear view over blue water
a red sunset
a dry handkerchief
and a kind word.
I long for a return of feeling
a flash of passion
a moment of joy.
I long to see Princess Diana
at the curb, her long legs
not mangled in a senseless crash
but gracefully stepping
out of a Mercedes
into a tangle of Queen Anne's Lace
waving in a soft wind.
I want her blue eyes
and her romantic heart
to be close to the moonlight
so hard-earned for each of us.
I long for a new door
opening to an orderly house.

HOMAGE TO THE PHOTOGRAPHER
— for Gus Gustafson

We stand at the entry of a cavernous arena.
The atmosphere is cobalt blue. Lights are few.
      Wearing a dark coat, he halts
      just inside the door.
Let's go in, I urge. Let's go.
 We are hobbled by his chant.
      I don't want to go. I don't want to go.
Let's go in. I have two tickets. Let's go.
      I don't want to go. I do not want to go.

Gracefully he backs away and quietly
disappears into the cobalt atmosphere.
A bare bulb casts scant light on the empty
boxing ring. The crowd does not roar.

Outside, the crows are silent.
Traffic on First Avenue has stopped.
In the city park, skaters glide.
The red sky at sundown grows pale.

In this cavernous hall we are left
to weep and wonder who
will capture the next
      decades of our evolution.

To Mark a Graceful Dance Well Done
– for Doris Seign

In a garden lush with pink impatiens
we linger at tea. Reminisce.
In an earlier time
she held a brand new baby girl
her sixth born
sat at her kitchen table
after dinner
and before baths she said,
"I don't think I can get up."

In some essential way
we are always speaking truth
to each other, sending each other's
heart rates up and down.

She did get up
began to hum a sonata
embraced her fierce need for beauty
packed courage in delicate layers
made an adagio leap from her kitchen
onto a racing train
and never looked back.
Her dance grew ever more graceful,
ever more bold.

Suddenly it was time
for the tea things to be collected.
"Can't you stay?" she said.
"Are we in a hurry here?" she said.

In midsentence a window closed
on her garden lush with red impatiens.
The room went dark for some time,

but now, a flutter of bright
silk caught between window and sill
trembles in the summer wind
reaches for the moon.

The bells have begun to ring
and at a piano, someone
is playing her sonata.

Beauty In Unexpected Places

– for an Unknown Architect

A pipe hand railing
in a concrete parking ramp
girds the stairway,
climbs from level one to level two,
and continues on
in brilliant scarlet.
Its climb is straight and sure.
At each landing it turns,
confident of its beauty,
forms three perfect triangles
and ascends.
Its unexpected grandeur
takes my breath away
as it sings its silent song
of beginnings and endings
and how they trade places.
I am reassured to see
that a voluptuous union,
at just the right juncture,
adds strength.

ODE TO THE CRITIC

I am not
an angry woman.
Fuck you.

SONG

– for Rick And Sonia

In that lovely tempestuous time, just
at the beginning, even before the first touch,
when you recognize your destiny,
see its beauty, the endless possibilities,
you are extraordinarily happy.
The music was written just for you.

It is a time when lilacs are in bloom
and in the everydays to follow you will
remember this spring. The blossoms are
as profuse as they have ever been.
You are wrapped in a positive conscious choice
like a bird in flight when the air is warm

at sunrise. The sky shimmers. You dance
hand in hand through the square. You sing
your unbridled joy to passersby. You bow
to the persistence of memory. You see
its beauty. You know with certainty
you don't want to be anywhere else.

THE MUSIC OF
WHAT IS

The Music

– for Carol Hogard and Mary Pruitt, founders
of the first Women Studies program in America at
Minneapolis Community Technical College

A woman rises
in a room
as big as this city gets
and from a deep well in her heart
and with a catch in her throat
she speaks the song of Ntozake Shange
 "& now she stood a
reglar colored girl
fulla the same malice
livid indifference as a sistah
worn from supporting a wd be horn player
or waitin by the window…"

A woman speaks, a curtain rises
and in a room
as big as this city gets
the air fills with new music
born in a small house on the corner
born in offices and small shops
born in kitchens and dance clubs
born in jails and 24 hour cafes
born in a dark house
on the edge of the city.
A woman speaks
and this room fills with music

slowly and carefully composed
in the extraordinary struggle
that comes with enduring
that comes with surviving
that comes whenever a woman decides

to breathe life into her dreams
whenever a woman decides
to punch her way straight
through the sound barrier
whenever a woman decides
to hear the new music
the sweet notes that sound

new answers to old questions
new music that transports her sky
high delicately and with magic.
This is not a romance poem.
This is a love poem.
This is a poem of honor
and admiration and applause.
This is a poem that bows from the waist
to the women who built this room
barehanded
without a blueprint, with simple tools
and a battered truck loaded with grit.

This is a deep bow from the waist
to the women who kept the lantern lit
as they cleared boulders from a virgin lot
paced and plotted and planned
then turned the untrod soil
made it ready
poured concrete
pounded strong supports
persevered
and pushed open the doors
to let in the new music.
The sweet notes.

In overstuffed chairs in small
settled rooms officials preferred

easy listening sounds
stewed about the new music
clucked: This Won't
This Won't Work This Can't
Last This Might Upset This
Could Be This Could…
this is a deep bow from the waist
to the women who belted their song
as they poured and pounded
and borrowed and begged

to the women, brave as bulldogs
and pioneers who can tell you
nothing is free
who paid a price
pulled from their own pockets
to sing this new music
so loud so loud
they never heard: This Won't
This Won't This Can't.
They became as intuitive as twins
never stopped singing
and never looked back.

A woman whose voice
has grown stronger
in a room
as big as this city gets
finishes
the song of Ntozake Shange
and the holiness
of herself is released
she peels an orange
it is more than she can eat
and she passes parts of it
to her sisters.

The sweet juice
runs down her arms
and she remembers when she was
alone
in that dark house
on the edge
of the city
when she thought
she would
never
stop being hungry.

About the Author

Carol Connolly was born, raised and educated in the Irish Catholic section of Saint Paul, Minnesota. She has eight children. She began writing poetry at the age of forty. Connolly is Saint Paul's first Poet Laureate, a lifetime mayoral appointment. She has worked as a columnist for the *Saint Paul Pioneer Press, Mpls. St. Paul* magazine, *Star Tribune* poetry reviewer, and is *Minnesota's Journal of Law and Politics Hearsay* columnist. She curates a monthly Reading by Writers series, now in its 11th year. She has been a commentator for KARE Television, an NBC affiliate, performed in *What's So Funny About Being Female?* at the Dudley Riggs Theatre in Minneapolis, has served as co-chair of the Minnesota Women's Political Caucus, chair of the Saint Paul Human Rights Commission, and a Minnesota Racing Commissioner, founding the Commission's affirmative-action committee.

In 1991 and 1992 Revalyn T. Golde adapted and directed a stage production of *Payments Due* at the Ivar Theatre in Los Angeles. In 1993 and 1994 Larry Roupe directed productions for the Lyric Theatre in Minneapolis. The late C. Bernard Jackson, the producer of the Los Angeles production commented, "Hard as I've tried to rid myself of all the pork accumulated as a 'boy child', Carol Connolly comes along to remind me that were I to undergo an autopsy, they'd probably find an oink or two." Larry Roupe says of Payments Due, "I fell in love with the poems—the richness of humanity, the beauty, the absolute honesty. They're poems for anyone who's paying attention."